The Illustrated

FRENCH AND ENGLISH PRIMER.

NEW YORK:
A. S. BARNES & COMPANY,
51 JOHN-STREET.
1853.

NOTE.

We think this little book will be hailed with pleasure, and will convey to the young scholar both amusement and instruction; and should the contents be committed to memory, will prevent many an after blunder on the names and genders of nouns. It will be found to be a most comprehensive vocabulary, and being compiled by a Frenchman, its accuracy may be relied on. It is hoped that the desire so often expressed for a French and English, and a Spanish and English Primer, and also a Primer in the three languages combined, may be realized in these three little Books. The Publishers indulge the hope, that this effort may prove a useful addition to many a Nursery and School-room library.

The following are the different Titles:—

"*A French and English Primer, illustrated;*"

"*A Spanish and English Primer, illustrated;*"

"*A French, Spanish, and English Primer:*" also,

"*A German and English Primer.*"

FRENCH. (Français. Francés.)		ENGLISH. (Anglaise. Inglés.)
1.		**1.**
Les Fleurs.		*The Flowers.*
L'Oreille d'Ours.		*The Auricula.*
Le Bluet.		*The Blue Bell.*
Une Tulipe.		*A Tulip.*
Le Chèvre-Feuille.		*The Honeysuckle.*
Le Grenadille.		*The Passion-Flower.*
Un Vase.		*A Glass Vase.*
Un Tendre.		*A Tendril.*
2.		**2.**
Un Jet d'Eau.		*A Fountain.*
Des Bosquets.		*Groves.*
Un Rosier.		*A Rose Bush.*
Les Parterres.		*The Flower Beds.*
Les Allées.		*The Walks.*
Une Image.		*An Image.*
Le Temple.		*The Temple.*
Les Bords.		*The Borders.*
3.		**3.**
Le Jardinier.		*The Gardener.*
Le Jardin.		*The Garden.*
Le Terrain.		*The Mould.*
Une Bèche.		*A Spade.*
Les Pois		*The Peas.*
L'Arrosoir.		*The Watering Pot.*
Une Houe.		*A Hoe.*
Le Balai.		*The Broom.*

FRENCH. (Français. Francés.)	ENGLISH. (Anglaise. Inglés.)
4.	**4.**
Un Monsieur.	*A Gentleman.*
Les Cheveux.	*The Hair.*
Un Habit.	*A Coat.*
Une Veste.	*A Waistcoat.*
Les Pantalons.	*The Trowsers.*
Un Chapeau d'Opéra.	*An Opera Hat.*
Les Gants.	*The Gloves.*
Les Bottes.	*The Boots.*

5.	**5.**
Bureau de Négociant.	*Counting-House.*
Le Pupitre.	*The Desk.*
Les Livres.	*The Books.*
Le Clerc.	*The Clerk.*
Les Lettres.	*The Letters.*
Les Files.	*The Files.*
Le Tabouret.	*The Tabouret.*
L'Almanach.	*The Almanac.*

6.	**6.**
La Loi.	*The Law.*
L'Avocat.	*The Counsellor.*
Un Juge.	*A Judge.*
Un Plaidoyer.	*A Plea.*
La Perruque.	*The Wig.*
Le Rabat.	*The Band.*
La Robe.	*The Gown.*
Le Fief.	*The Fee.*

FRENCH. (Français. Francés.)		ENGLISH. (Anglaise. Inglés.)
7.		**7.**
La Tête.	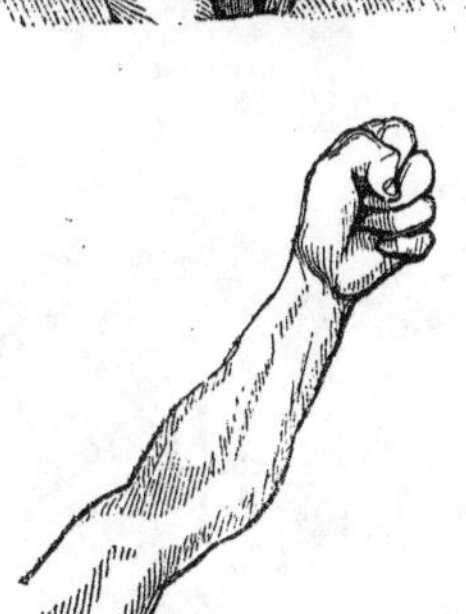	*The Head.*
Le Visage.		*The Face.*
Les Yeux.		*The Eyes.*
Le Nez.		*The Nose.*
La Bouche.		*The Mouth.*
Le Menton.		*The Chin.*
L'Oreille.		*The Ear.*
Le Sein.		*The Bosom.*
8.		**8.**
Le Bras.	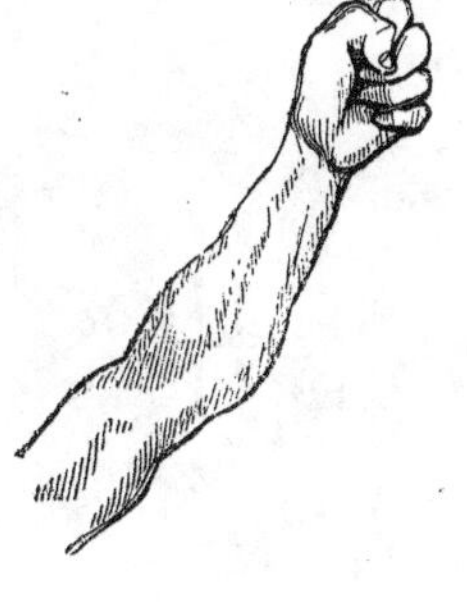	*The Arm.*
La Main.		*The Hand.*
Le Pouce.		*The Thumb.*
Les Doigts.		*The Fingers.*
Le Poignet.		*The Wrist.*
Les Ongles.		*The Nails.*
Les Muscles.		*The Muscles.*
Les Jointures.		*The Knuckles.*
9.		**9.**
La Jambe.	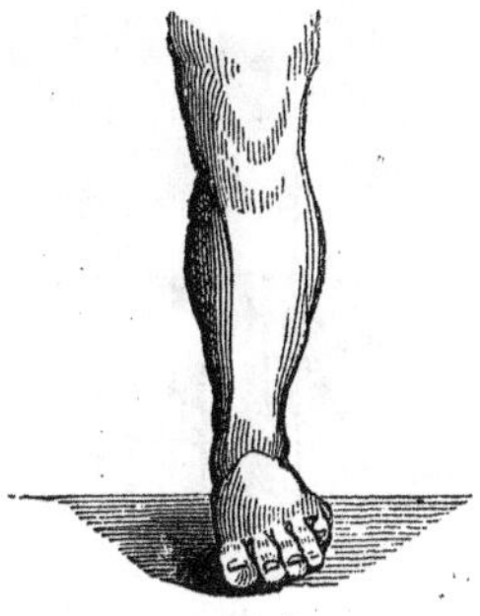	*The Leg.*
Le Pied.		*The Foot.*
La Cheville.		*The Ankle.*
Le Cou-de-Pied.		*The Instep.*
Les Doigts du Pied.		*The Toes.*
Le Mollet.		*The Calf.*
Le Genou.		*The Knee.*
La Peau.		*The Skin.*

FRENCH. (Français. Francés.)		ENGLISH. (Anglaise. Inglés.)
10.		**10.**
Un Maçon.		*A Bricklayer.*
Un Aide-Maçon.		*A Mason's Laborer.*
Les Briques.		*The Bricks.*
Le Mortier.		*The Mortar.*
La Truelle.		*The Trowel.*
Une Echelle.		*A Ladder.*
L'Echafaud.		*The Scaffold.*
Une Bêche.		*A Spade.*
11.		**11.**
Une Maison.		*A House.*
Le Front.		*The Front.*
Le Côté.		*The Side.*
La Porte.		*The Door.*
Les Pas.		*The Steps.*
Le Toit.		*The Roof.*
Les Cheminées.		*The Chimneys.*
Le Gazon.		*The Lawn.*
12.		**12.**
Une Fenêtre.		*A Window.*
Le Store.		*The Blind.*
Un Carreau.		*A Pane of Glass.*
Les Rideaux.		*The Curtains.*
Le Gland.		*The Tassel.*
Le Chassis.		*The Sash.*
L'Ombre.		*The Shadow.*
Le Mur.		*The Wall.*

FRENCH. (Français. Francés.)		ENGLISH. (Anglaise. Inglés.)

13.

La Cheminée.
Le Charbon.
La Fumée.
Les Pincettes.
La Pelle.
Le Fourgon.
Le Garde-Feu.

The Mantelpiece.
The Coal.
The Smoke.
The Tongs.
The Shovel.
The Poker.
The Fender.

14.

Une Citerne.
L'Evier.
Une Cruche.
La Cuve.
Les Poêlons.
La Grille.
Un Tamis.

A Cistern.
The Sink.
A Pitcher.
The Tub.
The Saucepans.
The Gridiron.
A Sieve.

15.

Une Cuisine.
Les Assiettes.
Les Plats.
La Cuisinière.
Un Panier.
Une Broche.
Une Four.
Le Dressoir.

A Kitchen.
The Plates.
The Dishes.
The Cook.
A Basket.
A Spit.
An Oven.
The Dresser.

FRENCH. (Français. Francés.)	ENGLISH. (Anglaise. Inglés.)
16.	**16.**
Bateau-à-Vapeur.	*Steamboat.*
Les Roues.	*The Paddles.*
L'Entonnoir.	*The Funnel.*
La Vapeur.	*The Steam.*
Les Mâts.	*The Masts.*
Le Gouvernail.	*The Rudder.*
Les Voyageurs.	*The Passengers.*
La Mer.	*The Sea.*

FRENCH.	ENGLISH.
17.	**17.**
Un Bateau-Pécheur.	*A Fishing-Boat.*
Les Pécheurs.	*The Fishermen.*
Les Voiles.	*The Sails.*
Les Filets.	*The Nets.*
Les Vagues.	*The Waves.*
Les Cordages.	*The Ropes.*
Les Nuages.	*The Clouds.*
Les Lièges.	*The Corks.*

FRENCH.	ENGLISH.
18.	**18.**
Un Matelot.	*A Sailor.*
Un Vaisseau.	*A Ship.*
La Mer.	*The Sea.*
Un Canon.	*A Cannon.*
Une Ancre.	*An Anchor.*
Une Pique.	*A Pike.*
Les Pistolets.	*The Pistols.*
Le Pont.	*The Deck.*

FRENCH. (Français. Francés.)		ENGLISH. (Anglaise. Inglés.)
19.		**19.**
Une Eglise.		*A Church.*
La Nef.		*The Nave.*
Les Ailes.		*The Aisles.*
Le Portique.		*The Porch.*
La Tour.		*The Tower.*
L'Horloge.		*The Clock.*
Les Pinnacles.		*The Pinnacles.*
Le Cimetière.		*The Churchyard.*
20.		**20.**
Un Pont.		*A Bridge.*
L'Arche.		*The Arch.*
Le Parapet.		*The Parapet.*
La Clef de Voûte.		*The Keystone.*
La Cascade.		*The Cascade.*
L'Ecume.		*The Foam.*
Le Saule.		*The Willow.*
Les Rochers.		*The Rocks.*
21.		**21.**
Un Château.		*A Castle.*
Les Murailles.		*The Walls.*
La Porte-Cochère.		*The Gateway.*
Les Tourelles.		*The Turrets.*
La Tour.		*The Tower.*
Les Créneaux.		*The Battlements.*
Le Pont-Levis.		*The Drawbridge.*
Le Fossé.		*The Moat.*

FRENCH. (Français. Francés.)	ENGLISH. (Anglaise. Inglés.)
22.	**22.**
Un Astronome.	*An Astronomer.*
Un Télescope.	*A Telescope.*
La Lune.	*The Moon.*
Les Etoiles.	*The Stars.*
Un Globe.	*A Globe.*
Une Comète.	*A Comet.*
Le Ciel.	*The Sky.*
Les Constellations.	*The Constellations.*

FRENCH.	ENGLISH.
23.	**23.**
Une Lampe.	*A Lamp.*
La Console.	*The Bracket.*
Une Chandelle.	*A Candle.*
Le Chandelier.	*The Candlestick.*
Une Bougie.	*A Wax Candle.*
Un Martinet.	*A Flat Candlestick.*
Les Mouchettes.	*The Snuffers.*

FRENCH.	ENGLISH.
24.	**24.**
La Lanterne Magique.	*The Magic Lantern.*
Les Rayons.	*The Rays.*
Le Tableau.	*The Painting.*
Le Disque.	*The Disk.*
La Lumière.	*The Light.*
La Lentille.	*The Lens.*
Le Medium.	*The Medium.*

FRENCH. (Français. Francés.)	ENGLISH. (Anglaise. Inglés.)
25.	**25.**
Insectes.	*Insects.*
Un Papillon.	*A Butterfly.*
Une Araignée.	*A Spider.*
Une Chenille.	*A Caterpillar.*
Une Mouche.	*A Fly.*
Une Sauterelle.	*A Grasshopper.*
Un Abeille.	*A Bee.*
Un Escarbot.	*A Beetle.*

FRENCH.	ENGLISH.
26.	**26.**
Un Cygne.	*A Swan.*
Le Bec.	*The Bill.*
Les Joncs.	*The Rushes.*
Les Ailes.	*The Wings.*
Les Plumes.	*The Feathers.*
La Queue.	*The Tail.*
La Rivière.	*The River.*
La Réflexion.	*The Reflection.*

FRENCH.	ENGLISH.
27.	**27.**
Un Nid d'Oiseau.	*A Bird's Nest.*
Les Œufs.	*The Eggs.*
Les Taches.	*The Spots.*
La Mousse.	*The Moss.*
Les Broussailles.	*The Sticks.*
Un Arbre.	*A Tree.*
Une Branche.	*A Branch.*
Les Feuilles.	*The Leaves.*

FRENCH. (Français. Francés.)	ENGLISH. (Anglaise. Inglés.)
28.	**28.**
Oiseaux.	*Birds.*
Un Aigle.	*An Eagle.*
Un Héron.	*A Heron.*
Un Coq.	*A Cock.*
Une Corneille.	*A Crow.*
Un Paon.	*A Peacock.*
Le Marais.	*The Marsh.*
Les Moineaux.	*The Sparrows.*

29.	**29.**
Animaux.	*Animals.*
Un Agneau.	*A Lamb.*
Un Ane.	*An Ass.*
Un Cheval.	*A Horse.*
Un Chien.	*A Dog.*
Le Pré.	*The Meadow.*
Le Bois.	*The Wood.*
L'Etang.	*The Pond.*

30.	**30.**
Le Chat.	*The Cat.*
Les Chatons.	*The Kittens.*
Un Tabouret.	*A Stool.*
Un Poële.	*A Pan.*
Le Lait.	*The Milk.*
Le Plancher.	*The Floor.*
Le Soufflet.	*The Bellows.*

FRENCH. (Français. Francés.)	ENGLISH. (Anglaise. Inglés.)
31.	**31.**
Des Jouets.	*Playthings.*
Un Cerf-Volant.	*A Kite.*
Les Etoiles.	*The Stars.*
Un Cerceau.	*A Hoop.*
Une Raquette.	*A Battledore.*
Un Sifflet.	*A Whistle.*
Les Volants.	*The Shuttlecocks.*
Un Sabot.	*A Whiptop.*

32.	**32.**
Un Ballon.	*A Balloon.*
L'Air.	*The Air.*
Le Char.	*The Car.*
Les Cordes.	*The Ropes.*
Les Aéronautes.	*The Aeronauts.*
Le Filet.	*The Netting.*
La Soie.	*The Silk.*
Les Drapeaux.	*The Flags.*

33.

33.	**33.**
Une Escarpolette.	*A Swing.*
Les Cordes.	*The Ropes.*
Le Banc.	*The Seat.*
Une Fille.	*A Girl.*
Un Garçon.	*A Boy.*
Une Robe d'Enfant.	*A Frock.*
Un Collet.	*A Collar.*
Un Ceinturon.	*A Belt.*

FRENCH. (Français. Frances.)	ENGLISH. (Anglaise. Inglés.)
34.	**34.**
Une Charrue.	*A Plough.*
Le Laboureur.	*The Ploughman.*
Le Soc.	*The Ploughshare.*
Les Chevaux.	*The Horses.*
Un Champ.	*A Field.*
Les Sillons.	*The Furrows.*
Un Fouet.	*A Whip.*
La Colline.	*The Hill.*

FRENCH.	ENGLISH.
35.	**35.**
La Moisson.	*The Harvest.*
Le Froment.	*The Wheat.*
La Paille.	*The Straw.*
Une Gerbe.	*A Sheaf.*
Les Moissonneurs.	*The Reapers.*
Une Faucille.	*A Sickle.*
Une Glaneuse.	*A Gleaner.*
Une Chaumière.	*A Cottage.*

FRENCH.	ENGLISH.
36.	**36.**
La Laiterie.	*The Dairy.*
Le Lait.	*The Milk.*
La Crême.	*The Cream.*
Le Beurre.	*The Butter.*
La Laitière.	*The Dairy Maid.*
La Baratte.	*The Churn.*
Les Terrines.	*The Milk Pans.*
L'Ecumoire.	*The Skimmer.*

FRENCH. (Français. Francés.)		ENGLISH. (Anglaise. Inglés.)
37.		**37.**
Une Boulangerie.		*A Bakehouse.*
Le Boulanger.		*The Baker.*
Le Four.		*The Oven.*
Un Pain.		*A Loaf.*
La Farine.		*The Flour.*
La Huche.		*The Kneading-Trough*
Une Pelle.		*A Shovel.*
Les Sacs.		*The Sacks.*
38.		**38.**
Un Apothicaire.		*An Apothecary.*
Une Pharmacerie.		*An Apothecary's Shop.*
Le Pilon.		*The Pestle.*
Le Mortier.		*The Mortar.*
Les Tiroirs.		*The Drawers.*
Le Comptoir.		*The Counter.*
Les Bouteilles.		*The Bottles.*
Médecine.		*Medicine.*
Le Médecin.		*The Doctor.*
39.		**39.**
Un Cordonnier.		*A Shoemaker.*
Les Souliers.		*The Shoes.*
Une Forme.		*A Last.*
La Courroie.		*The Strap.*
Le Cuir.		*The Leather.*
Un Pot à Fleurs.		*A Flower-Pot.*
Le Buffet.		*The Cupboard.*
La Cage.		*The Bird-Cage.*

FRENCH. (Français. Francés.)	ENGLISH. (Anglaise. Inglés.)
40.	**40.**
Tonnelerie.	*Coqperage.*
Un Tonnelier.	*A Cooper.*
Un Tonneau.	*A Cask.*
Une Doloire.	*An Adze.*
Les Cerceaux.	*The Hoops.*
Les Douves.	*The Staves.*
Une Cuve.	*A Vat*
Un Sceau.	*A Pail.*

FRENCH	ENGLISH
41.	**41.**
Un Ramoneur.	*A Chimney-Sweeper.*
Le Sac.	*The Sack.*
Les Brosses.	*The Brushes.*
La Suie.	*The Soot.*
Les Pieds.	*The Feet.*
Le Rattissoir.	*The Scraper.*
La Cabane.	*The Cottage.*
Le Grand Chemin.	*The High Road.*

FRENCH	ENGLISH
42.	**42.**
Un Coutelier.	*A Cutler.*
Une Roue.	*A Wheel.*
Un Maillard.	*A Grindstone.*
Une Courroie.	*A Strap.*
Une Epée.	*A Sword.*
Un Canif.	*A Penknife.*
Une Lancette.	*A Lancet.*
Les Patins.	*The Skates.*

FRENCH. (Français. Francés.)		ENGLISH. (Anglaise. Inglés.)
43.		**43.**
Un Forgeron.		*A Blacksmith.*
L'Enclume.		*The Anvil.*
Une Vis.		*A Vice.*
Le Soufflet.		*The Bellows.*
Les Pinces.		*The Pincers.*
La Forge.		*The Forge.*
Le Feu.		*The Fire.*
Un Gros Marteau.		*A Sledge Hammer*
44.		**44.**
Un Paveur.		*A Pavior.*
Une Pioche.		*A Pickax.*
Une Bêche.		*A Spade.*
Une Hie.		*A Rammer.*
Les Pierres.		*The Stones.*
La Rue.		*The Street.*
Un Ciseau.		*A Chisel.*
Une Ligne.		*A Line.*
45.		**45.**
Un Menuisier.		*A Carpenter.*
Le Banc.		*The Bench.*
Un Rabot.		*A Plane.*
Les Planches.		*The Boards.*
Une Scie.		*A Saw.*
Un Maillet.		*A Mallet.*
Le Carré.		*The Square.*
Des Copeaux.		*The Shavings.*

FRENCH. (Français. Francés.)		ENGLISH. (Anglaise. Inglés.)
46.		**46.**
Un Barbier.		*A Barber.*
Les Fers à Friser.		*The Curling-Irons.*
Les Ciseaux.		*The Scissors.*
Un Peigne.		*A Comb.*
Un Miroir.		*A Looking-Glass.*
Le Rasoir.		*The Razor.*
Le Buste.		*The Bust.*
Les Frisures.		*The Curls.*
47.		**47.**
Un Bourrelier.		*A Harness-Maker.*
Le Harnois.		*The Harness.*
Le Collier.		*The Collar.*
Les Rênes.		*The Reins.*
Les Etriers.		*The Stirrups.*
Les Traces.		*The Traces.*
Un Mors.		*A Bit.*
Une Selle.		*A Saddle.*
48.		**48.**
La Fileuse.		*The Spinner.*
Le Rouet à Filer.		*The Spinning-Wheel.*
Le Fuseau.		*The Spindle.*
Le Lin.		*The Flax.*
Le Fil.		*The Thread.*
La Toile.		*The Linen Cloth.*
La Maison.		*The House.*
Le Treillis.		*The Trellis.*

FRENCH. (Français. Francés.)		ENGLISH. (Anglaise. Inglés.)
49.		**49.**
Une Dame.		*A Lady.*
Les Plumes.		*The Feathers.*
Une Robe.		*A Gown.*
Un Collier.		*A Necklace.*
Un Bracelet.		*A Bracelet.*
Un Eventail.		*A Fan.*
Les Rubans.		*The Ribbons.*
Les Manchettes.		*The Ruffles.*
50.		**50.**
La Nourrice.		*The Nurse.*
Un Enfant.		*An Infant.*
Une Chaise.		*A Chair.*
Le Berceau.		*The Cradle.*
Un Marche-Pied.		*A Footstool.*
Le Bain.		*The Bath.*
Un Tablier.		*An Apron.*
Le Bassin.		*The Basin.*
51.		**51.**
Une Servante.		*A Housemaid*
Un Bonnet.		*A Cap.*
Un Torchon.		*A Mop.*
Un Balai		*A Broom.*
Un Sceau.		*A Pail.*
L'Eau.		*The Water.*
Le Pavé.		*The Pavement.*
Les Grilles.		*The Railings.*

FRENCH. (Français. Franoés.)	ENGLISH. (Anglaise. Inglés.)
52.	**52.**
Le Roi.	*The King.*
Le Diadème.	*The Crown.*
Le Sceptre.	*The Sceptre.*
Le Globe.	*The Globe.*
Le Trone.	*The Throne.*
La Jarretière.	*The Garter.*
Les Glands.	*The Tassels.*

FRENCH.	ENGLISH.
53.	**53.**
Une Chartre.	*A Charter.*
Les Mots.	*The Words.*
Les Lettres.	*The Letters.*
Les Cachets.	*The Seals.*
Le Parchemin.	*The Parchment.*
Cire à Cacheter.	*Sealing Wax.*
Le Chandelier.	*The Candlestick.*
Une Carte.	*A Map.*

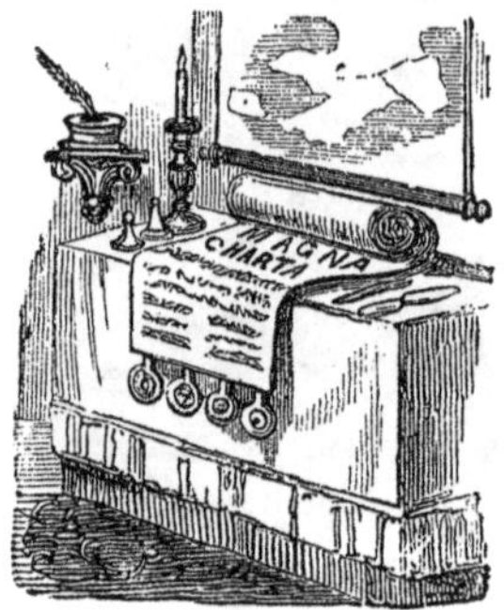

FRENCH.	ENGLISH.
54.	**54.**
Triomphe.	*Triumph.*
Une Victoire.	*A Victory.*
Les Bannières.	*The Banners.*
La Guirlande.	*The Wreath.*
La Croix.	*The Cross.*
La Frange.	*The Fringe.*
Un Guerrier.	*A Warrior.*
Le Casque.	*The Helmet.*

FRENCH. (Français. Francés.)	ENGLISH. (Anglaise. Inglés.)
55.	**55.**
Les Bohémiens.	*The Gypsies.*
Le Chaudron.	*The Caldron.*
Les Provisions.	*The Provisions.*
Le Lapin.	*The Rabbit.*
L'Oie.	*The Goose.*
L'Aube.	*The Ladle.*
Le Poêlon.	*The Saucepan.*
Le Bissac.	*The Bag.*

FRENCH.	ENGLISH.
56.	**56.**
Le Garde de la Forêt.	*The Woodman.*
Une Hache.	*An Ax.*
Une Serpe.	*A Billhook.*
La Forêt.	*The Forest.*
Le Moignon.	*The Stump.*
La Racine.	*The Root.*
L'Ecorce.	*The Bark.*
Le Fagot.	*The Fagot.*
57.	**57.**
Un Fermier.	*A Farmer.*
La Fauche.	*The Scythe.*
La Fourche.	*The Pitchfork.*
Le Rateau.	*The Rake.*
Le Fourgon.	*The Wagon.*
Le Faneur.	*The Haymaker.*
Le Foin.	*The Hay.*
Le Tas de Foin.	*The Hay-Stack.*

FRENCH. (Français. Francés.)	ENGLISH. (Anglaise. Inglés.)
58.	**58.**
Un Berger.	*A Shepherd.*
Les Claies.	*The Hurdles.*
Les Brebis.	*The Sheep.*
Le Fourrage.	*The Fodder.*
Un Agneau.	*A Lamb.*
Le Chien.	*The Dog.*
La Lanterne.	*The Lantern.*
La Houlette.	*The Crook.*

FRENCH.	ENGLISH.
59.	**59.**
Un Moulin a Vent.	*A Windmill.*
Le Meunier.	*The Miller.*
Les Voiles.	*The Sails.*
Les Marches.	*The Steps.*
Les Sacs.	*The Sacks.*
Du Grain.	*Corn.*
Du Blé.	*Wheat.*
La Farine.	*The Flour.*

FRENCH.	ENGLISH.
60.	**60.**
Une Laitière.	*A Milk-Maid.*
Les Sceaux à Lait.	*The Milking Pails.*
La Courge.	*The Yoke.*
Les Mesures.	*The Measures.*
Le Lait.	*The Milk.*
La Vache.	*The Cow.*
La Vacherie.	*The Cow-House.*
La Terre.	*The Ground.*

FRENCH. (Français. Francés.)	ENGLISH. (Anglaise. Inglés
61.	**61.**
Un Archer.	*A Bowman.*
L'Arc.	*The Bow.*
La Corde.	*The Bow-String*
La Flèche.	*The Arrow.*
La Pointe d'une Flèche	*The Arrowhead.*
Le Carquois.	*The Quiver.*
La Targe.	*The Target.*
L'Œil de Bœuf.	*The Bull's-Eye.*

62.	**62.**
Le Ménétrier.	*The Minstrel.*
Une Guitare.	*A Guitar.*
Les Cordes.	*The Strings.*
Le Pont.	*The Bridge.*
La Terrasse.	*The Terrace.*
La Montagne.	*The Mountain.*
Le Balcon.	*The Balcony.*
L'Entrée.	*The Entrance.*

63.	**63.**
Un Pécheur.	*An Angler.*
Une Baguette.	*A Rod.*
La Ligne.	*The Line.*
Un Hameçon.	*A Hook.*
Un Brochet.	*A Pike.*
Une Saule.	*A Willow.*
La Rive.	*The Bank.*
La Rivière.	*The River.*

FRENCH. (Français. Francés.)	ENGLISH. (Anglaise. Inglés.)
64.	**64.**
Les Courses.	*The Races.*
Les Spectateurs.	*The Spectators.*
La Galerie.	*The Stand.*
Les Chevaux.	*The Horses.*
Les Coureurs.	*The Jockeys.*
L'Herbe.	*The Grass.*
Les Rênes.	*The Reins.*
Le But.	*The Winning-Post.*

French	English
65.	**65.**
Le Chasseur.	*The Huntsman.*
Le Cor de Chasse.	*The Huntsman's Horn*
Un Cheval de Chasse.	*A Hunter.*
Une Barrière.	*A Gate.*
Le Chien.	*The Dog.*
Un Chemin.	*A Road.*
La Bride.	*The Bridle.*

French	English
66.	**66.**
Musique.	*Music.*
Un Tambour.	*A Drum.*
Une Flûte.	*A Flute.*
Les Cymbales.	*The Cymbals.*
Une Trompette.	*A Trumpet.*
Un Tambourin.	*A Tambourine*
Un Triangle.	*A Triangle.*
Une Clarinette.	*A Clarionet.*

FRENCH. (Français. Francés.)		ENGLISH. (Anglaise. Inglés.)
67.		**67.**
L'Hiver. Le Lac. La Glace. Les Glaçons. Les Patins. Les Patineurs. La Neige.		*Winter.* *The Lake.* *The Ice.* *The Icicles.* *The Skates.* *The Skaters.* *The Snow.*
68.		**68.**
L'Orage. La Grêle. La Pluie. Le Parapluie. Le Vent. Le Voile. La Haie. L'Herbe.		*The Storm.* *The Hail.* *The Rain.* *The Umbrella.* *The Wind.* *The Veil.* *The Hedge.* *The Grass.*
69.		**69.**
Chemin de Fer. Un Viaduc. Les Piles. Les Arches. Les Pierres. Les Briques. La Colline. La Vallée.		*Railroad.* *A Viaduct.* *The Piers.* *The Arches.* *The Stones.* *The Bricks.* *The Hill.* *The Valley.*

4

FRENCH. (Français. Francés.)	ENGLISH. (Anglaise. Inglés.)
70.	**70.**
Une Toilette.	*A Dressing-Table.*
Un Miroir.	*A Looking-Glass.*
Une Brosse à Cheveux.	*A Hair-Brush.*
Une Brosse à Dents.	*A Tooth-Brush.*
Un Peigne.	*A Comb.*
Une Pelote.	*A Pincushion.*
Les Epingles.	*The Pins.*
Un Flacon.	*A Glass Bottle.*

FRENCH.	ENGLISH.
71.	**71.**
Une Boîte de Carton.	*A Bandbox.*
Un Manchon.	*A Muff.*
Un Bonnet.	*A Lady's Cap.*
Un Chapeau de Femme.	*A Bonnet.*
Un Chale.	*A Shawl.*
Un Boa.	*A Boa.*
Une Ombrelle.	*A Parasol.*
Une Commode.	*A Chest of Drawers.*

FRENCH.	ENGLISH.
72.	**72.**
Déjeûner.	*Breakfast.*
Une Tasse.	*A Cup.*
Une Soucoupe.	*A Saucer.*
Une Cafetière.	*A Coffee-Pot.*
Un Pot au Lait.	*A Milk-Pot.*
Une Nappe.	*A Tablecloth.*
Un Coquetier.	*An Egg-Cup.*
Du Beurre.	*Butter.*

FRENCH. (Français. Francés.)		ENGLISH. (Anglaise. Inglés.)
73.		**73.**
Une Rose.	 	*A Rose.*
Un Rosier.		*A Rose-Tree.*
Les Boutons.		*The Buds.*
Les Epines.		*The Thorns.*
Les Feuilles.		*The Leaves.*
Les Fibres.		*The Fibres.*
Les Fleurs.		*The Blossoms.*
La Tige.		*The Stalk.*
74.		**74.**
Des Végétaux.		*Vegetables.*
Des Oignons.		*Onions.*
Des Carrottes.		*Carrots.*
Des Navets.		*Turnips.*
Un Chou.		*A Cabbage.*
Des Pommes de Terre.		*Potatoes.*
Des Pois.		*Peas.*
Des Concombres.		*Cucumbers.*
75.		**75.**
Du Fruit.		*Fruit.*
Un Ananas.		*A Pineapple.*
Les Raisins.		*The Grapes.*
Les Prunes.		*The Plums.*
Les Fraises.		*The Strawberries.*
Les Poires.		*The Pears.*
Les Pommes.		*The Apples.*
Une Pêche.		*A Peach.*

FRENCH. (Français. Francés.)		ENGLISH. (Anglaise. Inglés.)
76.		**76.**
La Vigne.		*The Vineyard.*
Les Raisins.		*The Grapes.*
Un Vigneron.		*A Vine-Dresser.*
La Vendangeuse.		*The Vintager.*
Les Paniers.		*The Baskets.*
L'Echelle.		*The Ladder.*
Un Echalas.		*A Wine-Press.*
Du Vin.		*Wine.*
77.		**77.**
Un Musée.		*A Museum.*
Un Vase Antique.		*An Antique Vase.*
Une Statue.		*A Statue.*
Une Médaille.		*A Medal.*
Les Livres.		*The Books.*
Les Brosses.		*The Brushes.*
Une Palette.		*A Pallet.*
Un Chevalet.		*An Easel.*
78.		**78.**
La Pompe.		*The Pump.*
La Manche.		*The Handle.*
Le Robinet.		*The Tap.*
La Cruche.		*The Pitcher.*
La Cour.		*The Yard.*
Le Judas.		*The Drain.*
Les Tuiles.		*The Tiles.*
Le Chaume.		*The Thatch.*

FRENCH. (Français. Francés.)		ENGLISH. (Anglaise. Inglés.)
79.		**79.**
Le Théâtre.		*The Theater.*
Le Rideau.		*The Curtain.*
Une Loge.		*A Box.*
Une Actrice.		*An Actress.*
Un Acteur.		*An Actor.*
L'Orchestre.		*The Orchestra.*
Les Coulisses.		*The Scenes.*
Les Lampes.		*The Lamps.*
80.		**80.**
Un Turc.		*A Turk.*
Un Cimeterre.		*A Cimiter.*
Une Pipe.		*A Pipe.*
Un Turban.		*A Turban.*
Le Croissant.		*The Crescent.*
Les Coussins.		*The Cushions.*
Les Pantoufles.		*The Slippers.*
La Mosquée.		*The Mosque.*
81.		**81.**
La Tablette.		*The Shelf.*
Un Rucher.		*A Bee Garden.*
Une Ruche.		*A Bee-Hive.*
Les Abeilles.		*The Bees.*
Les Fleurs.		*The Flowers.*
Rayon de Miel.		*Honeycomb.*
Le Miel.		*The Honey.*
La Cire.		*Bees' Wax.*

FRENCH. (Français. Francés.)		ENGLISH. (Anglaise. Inglés.)
82.		**82.**
La Porte de la Rue.		*The Street Door.*
Une Porte.		*A Door.*
Un Seuil.		*A Threshold.*
Les Jambages d'une [Porte.		*The Door-Posts.*
Un Marteau.		*A Knocker.*
Un Trou de Serrure.		*A Keyhole.*
Une Clef.		*A Key.*
Une Serrure.		*A Lock.*
83.		**83.**
Un Lit.		*A Bed.*
Un Bois de Lit.		*A Bedstead.*
La Colonne de Lit.		*The Bed-Post.*
Le Ciel de Lit.		*The Tester.*
Les Coins.		*The Cornices.*
Les Rideaux.		*The Curtains.*
Un Matelas.		*A Mattress.*
Les Oreillers.		*The Pillows.*
84.		**84.**
Une Montre.		*A Watch.*
Un Crochet.		*A Hook.*
Le Cadran.		*The Dial.*
Les Aiguilles.		*The Hands.*
La Boîte.		*The Case.*
La Chaîne.		*The Chain.*
Les Cachets.		*The Seals.*